CW00420921

PATHS AND PUBS OF THE WYE VALLEY

Twelve circular walks leading off the Wye Valley Walk between
Hereford and Monmouth, each featuring a halfway pub.

Revised Third Edition
by
HEATHER & JON HURLEY

Maps and drawings by David Grech, B.A., B. Arch., R.I.B.A.
Cover design by Doug Eaton.

ISBN 0 946328 31 5

Please respect the Country Code

Published by Infinite Design, Ross-on-Wye, 1998

CONTENTS

Dedication
Introduction

DEDICATION

To our children, Russell, Lawrence and Alice
who benefited from these walks.

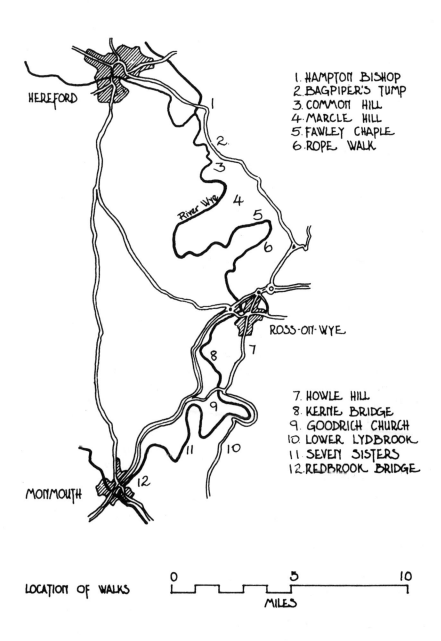

HEREFORD

1. HAMPTON BISHOP
2. BAGPIPER'S TUMP
3. COMMON HILL
4. MARCLE HILL
5. FAWLEY CHAPLE
6. ROPE WALK

River Wye

ROSS·ON·WYE

7. HOWLE HILL
8. KERNE BRIDGE
9. GOODRICH CHURCH
10. LOWER LYDBROOK
11. SEVEN SISTERS
12. REDBROOK BRIDGE

MONMOUTH

LOCATION OF WALKS

0   5   10

MILES

INTRODUCTION

By popular demand this walking guide of the Wye Valley has been revised for the third time. All of these interesting and varied circular routes which lead off the waymarked Wye Valley Walk, explore the unspoilt countryside between Hereford and the Welsh border town of Monmouth, and have been specially selected to feature a pub around the halfway point.

The Valley of the Wye is an Area of Outstanding Natural Beauty, where care is taken to conserve the countryside for the public's enjoyment. The tranquil Wye flows through this designated area on its way from the boggy mountains of Plynlimon in mid-Wales to join the Severn at Chepstow. The glorious Wye meanders on, chatteringly low at the height of summer, but dark and stormy, brimming with turgid flood water, in the rainy season. Farmers who live on its banks enjoy, as the Egyptians did when the Nile flooded, a precious inch or two of organic silt to help start their grass and crops growing with renewed energy the following spring.

On its way the great river, its belly full of fish, smoothly flows by the square grey pile above Mordiford where members of the Hereford family still live. Twisting back, almost mingling with its little sister the Lugg, it passes places with delightful Postman Pat names, like the three Greens; Sink, Fiddler's and Peartree. From here it sails past the modified remains of the once historic Aramstone, then on to Hoarwithy where the church of St. Catherine in all its odd but fascinating splendour peers down with its Tuscan tower. Llanfrother on the hill, where monks centuries ago plied their patient crafts, is next, then horseshoeing round to Sellack it slips under the bouncy suspension bridge below Caradoc, an Elizabethan mansion now undergoing renovation since being burnt down.

Next, past another attractive stretch at the quaintly named Hole-in-the-Wall, before sailing between the legs of a shattered railway bridge at Backney, where pillars built with Victorian skill and formidable craftsmanship still defy the river's moods.

At Brampton Abbotts the upper tiers of Ross are now within sight and the river laps the crumbling shell of Wilton Castle after making it's much photographed curve under the eaves of Ross. Cubberley next, where a fine old house has been replaced by what may become a modern classic of architecture, and on to the more traditional, more easily accepted Hill

Court, its majestic front turned away from the river. Rapidly now the Wye passes under the considerable shadow cast by the ample remains of Goodrich Castle, near to the ancient Flanesford Priory, now like many failing Wye Valley properties, bolstered by new money.

On to Courtfield, still occupied by priests, below Coldwell Rocks, wriggling around Symonds Yat to be gawked at by the throngs that occupy the rock every day of the year, especially now the Peregrine Falcons have become an annual floorshow. On the river flows, beside the newly accessible Coppet Hill, like its name, rusty in autumn with its bracken tinged with browns and ambers. Then far below the lofty Kymin where buckish young gentlemen disported themselves two hundred years ago. Under the seventeenth century stone arched bridge at Monmouth, relentlessly flowing on to its meeting with the Severn at Chepstow. Truly a great river, and one that fishermen, farmers, canoeists and ramblers will hopefully bless for centuries to come.

The Wye Valley Walk, waymarked with a leaping salmon logo, is a long distance path of one hundred and fifty miles leading from Chepstow to Rhayader. Throughout its length it closely follows the river, either beside its lush banks or above it following well worn hilly paths through thick wooded slopes. The condition of the paths has improved (any footpath problems should be reported to the relevant authority) since the first edition, thanks to more regular usage, and the elbow grease dispensed by stalwarts from the Countryside Service, and County Councils.

The pubs too have improved, many of them are Free Houses, owned, occupied and managed by families and are among the best. Several have changed hands since we last visited, but most 'new brooms' are as good, if not better, than the originals. Menus have become more interesting, the accent being on home made, using fresh ingredients. Vegetarians, once pariahs, now have a section of most menus to themselves, and wine lists are getting longer and more adventurous too.

Pubs are more reflective places now, with less of the electric noises associated with the goggle-eyed bandits which greedily gobble up small change while emitting ear piercing sounds. Children are catered for, and even under our archaic licensing laws, provisions are made for youngsters who if with their parents, can sip a soft drink and eat a sandwich in a side room. Sitting outside is a real treat in summer, and most of the pubs in this book excel in this department. The Hope and Anchor steals the show with its beautiful riverside setting, but the Butcher's Arms, the Lough Pool, the

Crown and the Green Man are not far behind. Live fires in winter are traditional and welcoming, and most of our inns provide this essential ingredient. When soggy after a rain swept walk there is nothing more pleasant than steaming by a crackling log fire with a drink, a bowl of good home-made soup and a 'toastie'. Loos are important, and they score highly in our pubs. All twelve inns are different, some walkers will favour one more than another, a few are for the job in hand, while some would grace any pub guide in the country.

Walkers please note, these rambles may vary slightly according to season, and changes made by the land users. Lanes, tracks, footpaths, bridlepaths and byways are followed where the public have a right of way. It is advisable, however, to refer to the relevant Ordnance Survey Sheet, where all Rights of Way are clearly shown. Other items required on these walks are sensible footwear, lightweight waterproofs and a rucksack to carry a map, compass, first aid and money for refreshments.

While enjoying the countryside,
please remember the Country Code;

- Enjoy the countryside and respect its life and work.
- Guard against all risk of fire.
- Fasten all gates.
- Keep dogs under close control.
- Use gates and stiles to cross fences, hedges and walls.
- Leave livestock, crops and machinery alone.
- Take litter home.
- Help to keep all water clean.
- Protect wildlife, plants and trees.
- Take special care on country roads.
- Make no unnecessary noise.

1. HAMPTON BISHOP

3½ mile walk from Mordiford Church
to the Bunch of Carrots.

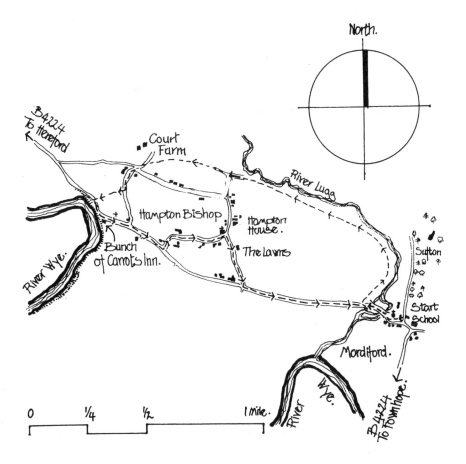

This is a leisurely stroll suitable for all ages, and can be equally enjoyed in mid-summer or in the depths of winter. Mordiford is a compact village with a church, old rectory, inn, shop and cottages neatly set between the hills of Haugh Wood and the banks of the River Lugg, a tributary of the nearby Wye. From the church at Mordiford the Wye Valley Walk is followed along the banks of the Lugg to the attractive village of Hampton Bishop, where the comforts of the inn can be sampled before returning.

Route

This gentle walk starts from the church at Mordiford (GR 571375) where parking is available. Opposite the church observe the Victorian school, opened in 1873, and still in use. Walk through the lych gate under the overhanging branches of an old yew tree, to the church dedicated to the Holy Rood. The Norman doorway remains, but the tower was rebuilt in 1811 replacing a central tower on which a twelve foot green dragon with a red mouth and tongue was painted in the fourteenth century to illustrate a local legend.

Leave the graveyard by the smaller gate, pass the entrance to the old rectory, now converted into several dwellings, and cross the River Lugg by a fine arch bridge dating back to the fourteenth century. Here the Wye Valley Walk is joined and the distinctive yellow arrows indicate the way. From Mordiford Bridge pleasant views can be seen of the village, the wooded hills, and Sufton, a large eighteenth century house. The waymarks lead to the right along the flood bank of the Lugg to the end of this large field where, to the right, buildings of Sufton and Old Sufton with its walled garden and dovecote will be seen. Ahead, are the church and houses of Hampton Bishop, surrounded by lovely countryside, marred only by pylons in this particular spot.

The Wye Valley Walk leaves the willow lined Lugg and turns left into the village to meet Rectory Road, but our way continues ahead through fields, over gates and stiles until reaching a farm track at Court Farm. Here turn left then right passing thatched black and white cottages and several modern houses. In winter the naked trees in the orchards and gardens provide useful sustenance for hungry blackbirds and fieldfares. Continue along a narrow footpath on the right, over a stile, and through a level paddock where a further stile leads to the Hereford to Fownhope Road. Cross the road carefully, to reach the Bunch of Carrots Inn.

The Bunch of Carrots Inn

The Carrots gets its unusual name, according to local legend, from an exclusive salmon pool in the nearby Wye. It has been an inn for at least one and a half centuries and recently considerably altered with multiple rooms and cosy snugs. it is comfortable, warm and well furnished with the walls covered in a most eclectic selection of pictures, everything from military scenes and bird prints to amusing fishing sketches.

Oak beams abound and there is a fire, a most welcoming sight for the freezing rambler, with plenty of room for stretching tired legs. The menu lists international snacks ranging from Icelandic Prawns, Cannelloni, Mexican burgers, Quiche Lorraine, Scotch Eggs and Murphy's Deep Pie to soups, chicken casserole, paté, scampi and plaice served with chips.

There is also a splendid carvery as well as 'dishes of the day' and a nice line in puds. The beers include Courage, Directors, Hook, Bass and Boddingtons and a fine array of malt whiskies. Average quality wine may be purchased by glass or bottle.

Muzak wafts soothingly and the service is swift and friendly. The Carrot is an interesting, comfortable and relaxing place for walkers, drivers or anyone else for that matter. Children are welcome and there is parking.

Return

A longer alternative now available is to follow the signed footpath leading from the inn. It leads along the banks of the Rivers Wye and Lugg for three and a half miles to Mordiford Bridge.

Otherwise leave the inn by turning right along the road towards Mordiford. After passing the former Methodist Chapel, take the second turning on the left called Whitehall Road which winds around pretty thatched cottages before reaching Hampton Bishop Church. Well kept, the church, dedicated to St. Andrew, has an unusual timbered tower and is worth a visit to see Norman remains, fifteenth century rereads, Jacobean pulpit and interesting monuments. From the church gate cross the road and follow the right hand fork leading in front of The Lawns, a Georgian brick built house with its outbuildings converted into cottages. Soon the Hereford to Fownhope Road is met, where a left turn is taken. A short stretch along this busy route will lead back across the Lugg to Mordiford Church.

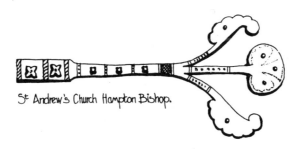

St Andrew's Church Hampton Bishop.

**5 mile walk from Fownhope
to the Moon Inn, Mordiford.**

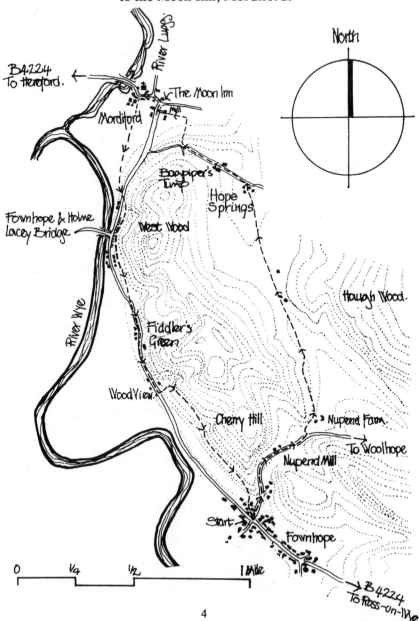

This picturesque ramble takes in some prettily named places: Hope Springs, Bagpiper's Tump, Fiddler's Green and Cherry Hill. The section along the Wye Valley Walk leads through a delightful valley before reaching the Moon Inn at Mordiford, and the return route along wooded hillsides offers outstanding views of the Wye.

The Drinking Fountain, Fownhope, erected in 1897.

Route

The walk begins from the minor crossroads at Fownhope (GR 572346) where cars can be parked by the roadside. There is a daily bus service from Hereford. From the crossroads follow the Woolhope Road and notice on the right hand corner a drinking fountain, erected in 1897 to commemorate Queen Victoria's Diamond Jubilee The road shortly passes the disused mill at Nupend, and a little further on, the Wye Valley Walk is joined. Turn left and follow the waymarked path through the gates and above Nupend Farm, where the track leads into wide fields through a broad open valley with the wooded hill of Haugh Wood on the right and mixed woodland of Cherry Hill, Fownhope Park and West Wood to the west.

A couple of isolated cottages are passed before reaching a farm track leading to barns and sheds at Hope Springs. The waymarks clearly direct a turn to the left, along a lane passing pretty cottages at Bagpiper's Tump. Bear right over the stile into a neat orchard where the tower of Mordiford Church comes into view. A further stile leads out of the orchard into the yard of a tall old mill, which still boasts the rusting remains of its water wheel. On reaching the road turn right, where the Moon Inn will be seen ahead.

The Moon Inn

The Moon is a fifteenth century stone and wood local with two neat bars and a garden for sitting out on sunny days. It enjoys good views of the surrounding hills. The village of Mordiford is attractive with clusters of brick and stone cottages and the old mill.

The Moon is a Whitbread Partnership pub with Wadsworth 6X and Boddingtons on tap and a large but inexpensive menu of excellent snacks and substantial fish dishes. The wine list is cheap and acceptable. Sundays, traditional roasts are available

The interior is attractive and the landlord has done much to improve matters. Walkers will find this a useful stop.

Return

Mordiford's thirteenth century church, fourteenth century bridge and Georgian rectory can be viewed before returning along the Ross Road. Within a few yards turn right following the Wye Valley Walk until reaching a stile on the left. Follow the field path ahead over stiles and upon reaching the road turn right. Opposite the next cottage climb a signed footpath to a forest track, where a right turn is taken. Here one sees the first fine views of the Wye, twisting and turning in the valley below, spanned here by the modern Fownhope and Holme Lacy Bridge constructed in 1973, replacing a former iron structure. The forest track continues until descending to the road just before Fiddler's Green. Follow the road to the left past a few impressive houses, including Morney Cross, Wood View and Rock House. Beyond the latter a signed footpath on the left through a field is followed alongside the boundary of the terraced gardens of Rock House.

At the corner of the field, go through the gate and turn immediately right. From here the path is more clearly defined, skirting the wooded hills with a fence on the right hand side. In springtime violets, primroses, bluebells and wood anemones are seen in abundance in these woods, again the views of the Wye are quite outstanding On reaching the new houses at Fownhope, continue behind gardens and within 100 yards turn right over a stile into a small housing estate. Follow the road to the main Fownhope Road, where a left turn brings you back to the crossroads.

3. COMMON HILL

3½ miles around Fownhope
to the Green Man Inn.

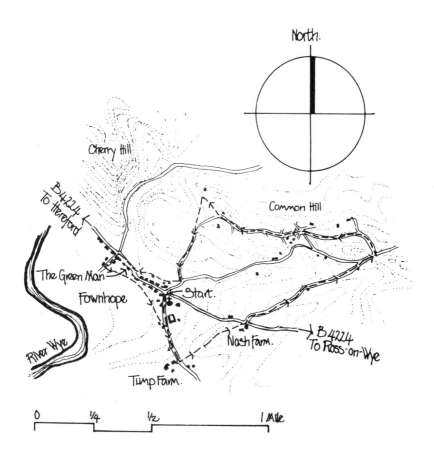

Fownhope lies between the meandering Wye and the irregular wooded slopes of Common Hill. The expanding village has a thriving community, centred along the route of the old Hereford to Gloucester Road, where shops, inns, a school and a beautiful Norman church are conveniently situated. This ramble follows paths and lanes leading to Common Hill where the Wye Valley Walk is joined. Extensive views may be appreciated from the hill before descending to the Green Man Inn at Fownhope.

Route

Fownhope Church (GR 581343) is our starting point. Cars can be parked in the village. St. Mary's Church is worth a visit, with its well preserved Norman tympanum, amongst other historical items on display in this spacious building with its fourteenth century tower and spire.

The Norman Tympanum in Fownhope Church.

Follow the lane behind the church towards Capler, passing some interesting houses of varied architectural styles. At the top of the hill, opposite Tump Farm situated in a prominent position, turn sharp left up the steep steps, over a stile and into fields. Suddenly there are fine views of Fownhope, Haugh Woods, Holme Lacy, Capler Hill and the Valley of the Wye. Keep to the left until reaching the leaning stone wall surrounding Nash Farm. Bear left here over a stile, then turn right, passing the elegant red brick Georgian farmhouse, before joining the road at a gate.

Cross the Fownhope to Ross Road and follow the quiet Hawker's Lane ahead, leading gently up to Common Hill. In springtime the banks between the pretty cottages are covered with snowdrops, violets, primroses and daffodils. The views are ever changing as you climb to over 500 feet. Just beyond an attractive white washed cottage the waymarks of the Wye Valley Walk are followed to the left, through the cottage drive, slightly left, then across a well made stile to follow a sunken green lane, probably used for transporting lime from the numerous lime pits on Common Hill. The waymarked path crosses an open area called Monument Hill, now a nature reserve, where the limestone grassland attracts many gaily coloured butterflies during summer. A further stile is crossed, and here a well defined track leads to a clearing where a network of paths and lanes meet. Continue following the Wye Valley Walk across the ridge of Common Hill.

Before descending, a black and white cottage is passed on the right. This is where one leaves the Wye Valley Walk to follow a track on the left, going downhill through the trees, then across a field, where a further track is joined leading down to the outskirts of Fownhope. At a new housing estate go right along Church Croft, and follow the paved path between bungalows to Court Orchard. Beside the village school and its large sign follow the footpath on the left leading onto the main road, where the Green Man will be seen on the right.

The Green Man

The Green Man buzzes during lunchtimes, an encouraging sign for the hungry walker. Built in the fifteenth century, it retains some old style charm. There are two bars, the main one spacious, oak beamed and relaxing with a fire to toast the winter walker. The menu is extensive, listing substantial snacks and full blown fare too, everything from the dish of the day to trout in almonds, soups, steaks and fish and an extensive sweet trolley. Veggies are catered for. The beer is good with several Real Ales on tap. These include Pedigree, Courage, Directors and Hook Norton, as well as the usual Beamish and Guinness, lagers with long German names and several farmhouse ciders. The wine list is adventurous by pub standards. Service is efficient and the atmosphere friendly. Customers include the tweeds and Telegraph variety, a good mixture of youngsters and the rustic chat club; a good pub attracts all sorts. An item of interest to pugilists is that the legendary Tom Spring, a tough, bare knuckle bruiser and once heavy weight champion of all England in 1823 was not just born in Fownhope but is said to have done a stint as landlord at the Green Man - he didn't but it's a good story! There are reception and banqueting facilities, accommodation, playground, garden and good parking facilities.

Return

After refreshments, continue along the road towards Hereford to a minor crossroads. Take the left turning to Ferry Lane, which as the name suggests leads to the River Wye. Up to the 1920's a boat carried travellers across the river to Holme Lacy. Opposite the Forge and Ferry Inn follow a signed path, cross a brook and continue to the left, around the side of a large field. Walk behind inns and houses where glimpses of the Wye may be seen. Another brook and stile is crossed leading onto a football pitch. At the next cottage turn left through the gates, where a short stretch along the road to the left leads back to Fownhope Church.

**12 mile walk from Brockhampton
to the Butcher's Arms, Woolhope.**

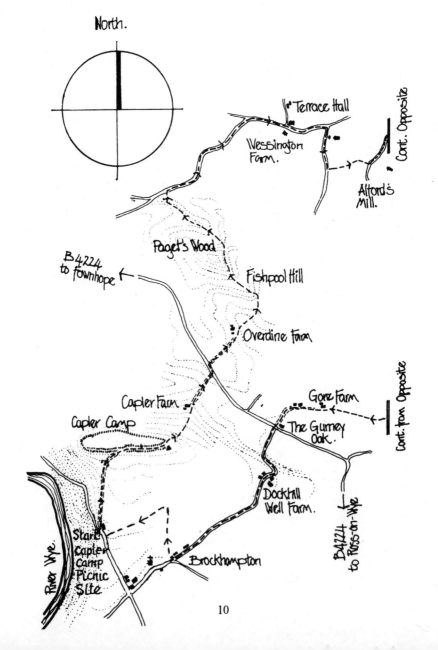

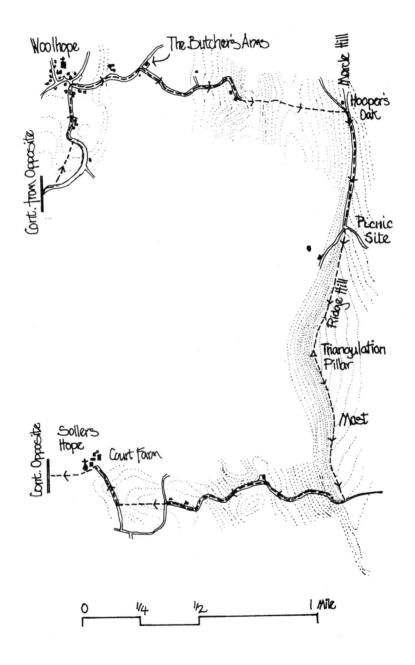

Woolhope

The Butcher's Arms

Marcle Hill

Hooper's Oak

Cont. from Opposite

Picnic Site

Ridge Hill

Triangulation Pillar

Mast

Sollers Hope

Court Farm

Cont. Opposite

| 0 | ¼ | ½ | 1 Mile |

This superb walk combines everything, from an Iron Age hillfort at Capler, an eighteenth century lime kiln at Woolhope, to the towering modern TV mast on Ridge Hill. Quiet lanes, pleasant paths, and the Wye Valley Walk, lead from the scenic picnic site at Capler across rolling hills to Woolhope, before returning along the ridge from Much Marcle to Sollers Hope. Spectacular views of the Malvern Hills and the Black Mountains may be enjoyed and admired throughout this longer walk, and it is worth the effort to visit The Butcher's Arms at Woolhope.

Lime Kilns on the approach to Marcle Hill

Route

Parking is available at Capler Picnic Site, (GR 591323) but before bearing right to follow the Wye Valley Walk, glance left to one of our favourite views of the River Wye. Cross the road to follow the waymarked path along a track, then diagonally across a conifer plantation, and turn right when reaching the double ramparts of Capler Camp, an Iron Age fort standing at 600 feet, with magnificent views.

An isolated cottage and barn at Capler are passed before bearing sharp left down a flight of wooden steps. The way continues ahead through fields and over stiles then left to arrive at the lane serving Capler Farm. A right turn leads to the main Ross to Fownhope Road, which is followed to the left for a few yards. Another right turn to Overdine Farm is clearly indicated, where the waymarked path leads through fields around the farm, up Fishpool Hill to Paget's Wood and needs to be carefully followed.

Paget's Wood is sixteen acres of mixed woodland owned by the Herefordshire Nature Trust. The walk through the nature reserve is quite delightful, with a great variety of wild flowers and small birds in abundance. The limestone of the Woolhope Dome has now been reached, and the first disused lime kilns will be seen in this wood, almost hidden by debris. A lovely open valley leads across to a tarmaced lane, which is followed to the right leaving the route of the Wye Valley Walk.

After about half a mile of bends and hills, keep right at the next junction to pass the attractive black and white buildings of Terrace Hall standing opposite Wessington Farm. Take the next right hand lane and within 500 yards follow a bridleway through a field gate. It leads parallel along the banks of a brook meeting a lane leading to Alford's Mill. Turn left along the lane and beyond a right hand bend, turn left over a stile, where a field path leads ahead over a footbridge and across a meadow to join a tarmac lane. Bear left towards Woolhope, which is soon reached.

Woolhope lies in an elevated position, and contains a pleasing mixture of stone and brick buildings clustered around a church dedicated to St. George dating from the early thirteenth century. Standing next to the church is the popular Crown Inn but if you do not wish to explore the village, turn right immediately at the village along the tarmac lane leading to the Butcher's Arms, lying a little distance from the village in a most delightful setting.

The Butcher's Arms

This pleasant and deservedly popular inn compliments an excellent walk. Set amid attractive farmland with a stream trickling through the small garden. With its low beam ceilings, cosy atmosphere and log fires in winter, it is the ideal place to slip away from the bustle of modern living. While a modern extension has been added it does not detract from the pub in any way. Old bar furniture and a profusion of Dendy Saddler prints help create the right ambience.

The menu is good, satisfying and imaginative with the excellent Woolhope Pie, Mushroom Biriani, homemade Steak and Kidney Pies, salads, sandwiches and soups at reasonable prices. The beers include such reputable draught ales as Bass, Old Hookey and Marston's Pedigree, and there is a sensibly chosen wine list. A more comprehensive evening menu caters for diners who are prepared to make the trip to this little black and white fourteenth century pub.

Happily no sounds other than the whistling of birds in the fields outside intrude to spoil the harmonious atmosphere, and a sealed off public bar caters for the sporting element, who can chuck darts and quoits to their heart's content. Outside jaded walkers may sit in the shade and take their well earned repast in idyllic comfort, before setting off for the second, and equally searching, part of this fine walk.

Return

Drag yourself away from the inn by following the narrow lane alongside the car park, crossing the brook that runs through the pub's garden. This old lane steeply ascends the wooded hill and turns sharply right before passing an isolated dwelling, after which a gate leads onto open hillside where well preserved lime kilns can be investigated. At over 500 feet panoramic views of the Herefordshire countryside and the Black Mountains may be savoured. The well defined track leads down the left hand side of a small wood. The path then continues in a straight line through fields, descending, then climbing, to the roadside opposite Hooper's Oak at the southern end of Marcle Hill.

A right turn along the road is the start of the scenic ridge walk, over-looking Ledbury and the Malvern Hills from a height of over 800 feet. At the next road junction beside a picnic site keep straight ahead up stone and earth steps, cross the stile and continue along Ridge Hill.

The path leads over stiles, through fields, then along an enclosed path, past the triangular pillar and the TV mast supported by huge cables. A little further on the path descends to a wooden stile in the corner of a field when it meets a sunken track. Turn right here gradually descending through woodland and past several barns. More disused lime kilns may be seen on the right. At the top of the kiln a large pit lies above the furnace holes, where fired lime was produced from layers of coal and limestone. Before crossing a brook the track becomes tarmaced, winding its way down to meet a lane at Sollers Hope.

Cross the lane and enter the field opposite by the gate, and follow an undefined path straight across the field to Church Lane. Turn right towards the secluded church standing next to Court Farm, an attractive sixteenth century black and white building. Keep left of the fourteenth century church at Sollers Hope and continue through the graveyard to the metal gate where a waymarked path leads from the footbridge straight across a field. At the next stile continue ahead keeping to the left hand side through two fields. Ignore the next stile ahead and turn sharp left over a stile and proceed in the same direction around Gore Farm. Within a few hundred yards a stile on the right leads into an unmade lane leading past cottages to reach the main road beside the former Gurney Oak inn.

Cross the road, follow the narrow winding lane up past Dockhill Well Farm, and within a mile turn right at the telephone box, or keep ahead to visit Brockhampton Church built in 1902 epitomising the spirit of the Arts and Crafts movement. From the telephone box the path leads along a track to a cottage. Bear diagonally right through the field to a stile, and continue in the same direction to the next stile. Here turn sharp left along the field boundary to return to the picnic site at Capler Camp.

5. FAWLEY CHAPEL

**10 mile walk from Hole-in-the-Wall
to the Lough Pool Inn, Sellack.**

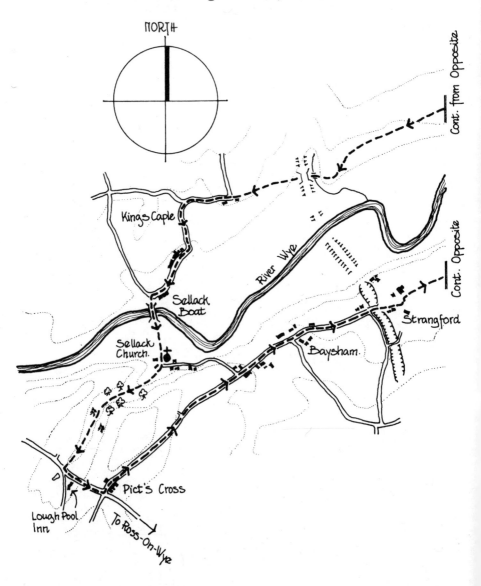

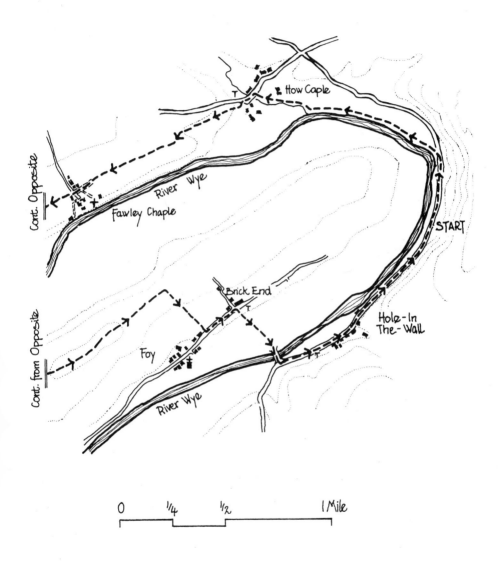

Cont. Opposite

How Caple

River Wye

Fawley Chaple

START

Cont. from Opposite

Brick End

Foy

Hole-In-The-Wall

River Wye

0   1/4   1/2   1 Mile

From a delightful stretch of the River Wye at Hole-in-the-Wall, footpaths and bridleways lead through the heart of the scenic Wye Valley to Sellack. Here the river is crossed by a swaying suspension bridge, then a delightful footpath is followed to the Lough Pool Inn. The return continues along lanes and paths offering splendid views in all directions of the Wye.

The Lough Pool Inn

Route

From the limited parking beside the Wye Valley Walk display board at Hole-in-the-Wall (GR 617295) proceed in a northerly direction following the waymarks to the banks of the Wye where, the riverside path eventually veers right alongside a brook to join the road at How Caple. From here to Kings Caple the route follows the line of an old Roman Road instead of the Wye Valley Walk. Turn left at the telephone box and through a gate across the field towards a house. Bear right keeping the field boundaries on the left until reaching a wooden hurdle, where the way continues in the same direction on the other side of the hedge. On approaching buildings cross a muddy farmyard and along a short track between houses to meet a tarmac lane at Fawley Chapel.

The Norman Chapel, neatly tucked away, can be seen on the left; our way however continues ahead along a little used but signed bridleway, through a series of gates across a yard. Keep to the right hand side of the

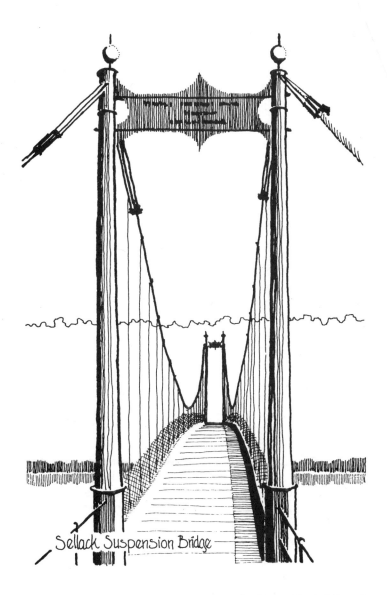

Sellack Suspension Bridge

fields until reaching a gate ahead, from here the line of the bridlepath goes straight across a large field towards a gate beside an oak. Cross the gate, keep close to the right hand hedge, pass the scanty remains of Mutloe's Barn then descend and bear right through a narrow gate. Cross a marshy brook by a concrete bridge beside a pool, then proceed ahead under a disused railway bridge. Now ascend through fields to Ingsbury Cottage at Kings Caple.

Follow the tarmac lane ahead, fork left at the junction and descend to cottages at Sellack Boat. At a sharp bend, turn left through a gate along a signed path leading to a suspension bridge spanning the Wye. This late nineteenth century construction replaced a former ferry. At the other side walk across the riverside meadows following a well used path to Sellack Church. This is the only English church dedicated to Celtic St. Tysilio who lived during the seventh century. The building has an unusual layout and contains many interesting monuments.

From the church turn left along a tarmac lane and within a few yards turn right across a stile to follow a signed footpath along the banks of a brook. At the end of the meadow cross another stile, bear slightly right through woodland lying above a group of fishponds from which the brook flows. Cross a stile out of the woods and continue up a delightful valley to reach a stile opposite the Lough Pool Inn.

The Lough Pool Inn

It is always a treat half way round a leisurely walk to see this little black and white Free House with its rustic seats and old cider press. The present owners have been in charge for a few years and a packed car park bears witness to the fine job they are doing in keeping both visitor and local fed and watered. Apart from the friendly welcome, and in winter the sweet smelling fire, the Lough Pool is spick and span with its stone flagged floors, old polished furniture and exposed beams. There is but one bar these days with a couple of nooks and adjoining dining room with accommodation for upwards of fifty diners. The menu, chalked on a blackboard, is always full of eye-catching grub, vegetarian and otherwise. Fish, meat and cheese dishes are attractively served with salads. The beer is always in good condition and Wye Valley Bitter, Bass, John Smith and the ubiquitous Caffreys are available. Wine is offered too and from a reasonably varied list a pleasant bottle of inexpensive red, white or pink can be chosen. Electrical gadgets are neither seen nor heard, and there is not even a dart board. Walkers and children are welcome, though the former might be asked to park their muddy footwear outside. But this is a small price to pay to enjoy one of the consistently finest pubs in Herefordshire.

Return

From the inn follow the road towards Ross, but at the top of the hill turn left at Pict's Cross along a pleasant tarmac lane for about one mile leading to Baysham and Strangford. Where the lane turns sharply right keep ahead along a lane crossing over the remains of the Hereford, Ross, Gloucester Railway line, where a deep cutting has been used as a landfill tip, now reinstated as a meadow. The stone walls of a former bridge are the only remainders of this railway. Pass some cottages before reaching a farmyard, here keep left of a pool and proceed along a ridge track following a waymarked path one side and then another of the field boundary until reaching a stile.

From this point the path is undefined after crossing the stile, continue in the same direction for about 200 yards then turn right over a stile in the hedge. Scramble over a tiny reservoir and descend a sloping field. Keep on the right and enter a farmyard before meeting the road at Foy.

Turn left along the road and opposite cottages at Brick End turn right following a signed and clearly defined footpath leading between fields to Foy suspension bridge. Linger awhile on this bridge to savour this wonderful stretch of the Wye where canoeists, fishermen, bird watchers and walkers enjoy an unspoilt and peaceful scene. A bridle bridge was first erected here in 1876, but was washed away by floods and replaced in 1921.

Having crossed the Wye turn left along a tarmac lane leading back past farms and cottages to Hole-in-the-Wall. After crossing a cattle grid return to the start within half a mile.

6. ROPE WALK

7½ mile walk from Hole-in-the-Wall to the Hope and Anchor Inn, Ross-on-Wye.

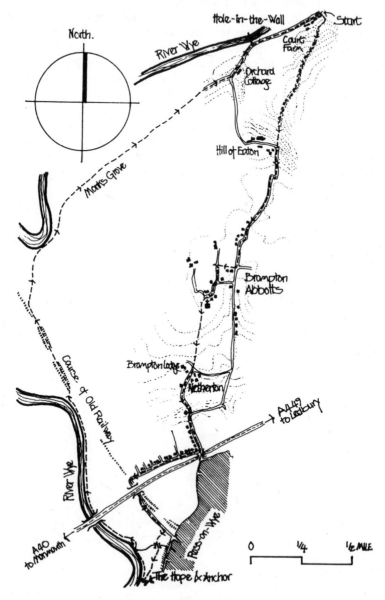

Hole-in-the-Wall refers to a collection of attractive cottages situated in Foy, a beautiful riverside parish divided by the meandering River Wye. Walkers can park their cars here before setting off across hills, along winding lanes and through the quiet village of Brampton Abbotts before reaching the market town of Ross-on-Wye and the Hope and Anchor Inn. The longer return route along the Wye Valley Walk closely follows the banks of the river.

Cottages at Hole-in-the-Wall in 1986

Route

Limited car parking is available at Hole-in-the-Wall (GR 611286). Follow the signed footpath 'Brampton Abbotts' which leads between a phone box and Aberhall Cottages. Where the footpath enters the field, turn right and walk uphill to the next gate, which leads onto a sunken lane passing behind Court Farm, now an Adventure Holiday Centre. This grassy track bears slightly to the left, leading steeply to another gate. At the top of this hill there are some splendid views of Foy with its old church and suspension bridge spanning the Wye. Now above an ancient L-shaped earthwork, the way continues ahead through fields, keeping to the left hand side until an enclosed path leads to an open field. Walk straight ahead where a steep climb leads to a stile beside a footpath sign, which can clearly be seen to the left of the farm buildings at Hill of Eaton.

Follow the tarmac lane to the left around the bends for about half a mile. On approaching Brampton Abbotts the wooded hills of Chase and Penyard beyond Ross become visible. At a road junction look out for the usual OS benchmark enclosed by iron railings, then turn right up steps, cross a stile and walk straight through the field towards a rendered cottage, once the village smithy. Continue ahead following the signed footpath through the orchard where the next stile leads onto a narrow metalled lane. Here turn left and at the bend keep ahead along a signed footpath to reach St. Michael's Church, Brampton Abbotts This neat building with its timber bell turret dates back to the Normans and has a pleasing fourteenth century porch. Proceed through the churchyard with its varied and interesting headstones and leave by the iron swing gate.

A well trodden path leads through fields, where the bustle of Ross-on-Wye can be heard. Shortly the farm and barns at Netherton are reached, continue ahead to follow a lane with the elegant Brampton Lodge on your right. Another uphill climb leads to the Brampton Road, followed right to the outskirts of Ross. Before the modern road bridge turn right along Greytree Road, leading down, around and under another bridge to meet Homs Road. A small playground is passed before reaching the Car Park on the right. Walk through this and cross the footbridge over Rudhall Brook. Keep ahead along the Rope Walk through the riverside meadows to the Hope and Anchor Inn.

The Hope and Anchor Inn

The Hope, as it is locally known, now a Banks's pub and recently renovated is attractively situated on a bend of the river, below Ross-on-Wye. A former innkeeper kept a pleasure boat for his clients' use, while another landlord regularly rowed downstream to collect withies near Wilton Castle, for his spare time occupation as a basket weaver. The present owners continue this watery connection and the aptly named Boat bar actually contains two boats. One, the Gypsy Queen, is now used as the counter but in its heyday transported holiday makers up and down this lovely stretch of river. The rowing boat which now hangs a little ignominiously from the ceiling once bulged with freshly netted salmon. To complete the nautical theme a small anchor, fished from the river by a diver some years ago, is displayed in the bar. A selection of sepia snaps of Ross by the riverside is a recent innovation. Easy 'listening' music is played and daily newspapers are available in the bar. Upstairs the Parlour is a comfortable book lined room with a Victorian flavour.

A friendly and casual pub, three hundred years old, the Hope offers a selection of both draught and bottled beers. These include the brewers range, Marston's Pedigree, Fosters, Harp and Strongbow Cider. The wine list is unimaginative but cheap. The menu is extensive and competitively priced, ideal ramblers fare with rich brothy soup, dish of the day specials as well as the usual beef, chicken and fish. For pud there is apple pie, Spotted Dick, steamed ginger sponge, rich chocolate cake and cream, with coffee to finish. Children and vegetarians are welcome and there is ample parking. The Hope enjoys spacious grounds with attractive river views which provide a pleasant spot for visitors and locals alike. A brass band plays in summer and the Morris Men cavort occasionally

Return

Leave the inn and walk to the rive bank, turn right to follow the Wye Valley Walk back to Hole-in-the-Wall. After re-crossing the Rudhall Brook, go around the boat house and under the modern river bridge; the path continues along the riverside for nearly a mile. This is a popular haunt for fishermen, swans, herons and wild ducks. The route bears right and follows a stretch of the disused Hereford, Ross, Gloucester Railway track, which operated between 1855 and 1964. The remaining hedgerows provide a useful habitat for wildlife. The waymarked path leaves the railway track as indicated before reaching Backney, where an iron memorial cross on the river bank may be seen. The waymarks lead on alongside a replanted wood called Monks Grove and continues through level pastures and fertile fields.

Opposite Foy Church, which is situated on the far side of the Wye, the path leads up to a gate, where a short track joins the road. turn left down the road passing the isolated Orchard Cottage, and observe on your left Foy Bridge built in 1921, replacing a former bridge washed away by heavy floods. Within a quarter of a mile the cottages at Hole-in-the-Wall will be reached.

Ross-on-Wye from across the river.

7. HOWLE HILL

**7 mile walk from Ross-on-Wye
to the Crown Inn, Howle Hill.**

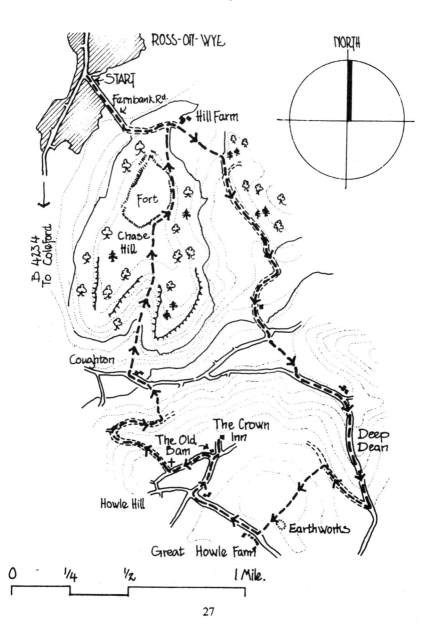

This is an energetic scenic ramble across the lovely wooded hills lying to the south of Ross-on-Wye. Starting from the town outskirts, a route of a former turnpike road, abandoned 200 years ago, is followed to Deep Dean where an ascent is made to Howle Hill offering panoramic views from its ancient earth work. The return is along the waymarked path of the Wye Valley Walk incorporating a stiff climb up Chase Hill.

Route

Park in Fernbank Road (GR 598232) a turning off the Walford Road lying to the south of Ross-on-Wye. From here to Deep Dean the walk follows the route of a former turnpike road, which because of being out of repair and inconvenient was abandoned at the end of the eighteenth century and replaced by an easier road. Fernbank Road becomes a track leading to Hill Farm, then proceed ahead between the farm and a bungalow, cross a stile and keep to the left hand side of a meadow. Before a solitary oak tree in the hedge turn left over a stile and within a few yards cross a further stile. Bear right following an uneven track gradually descending until reaching a stile. Cross this, but continue walking in the same direction along the forest track. Fork right beyond the hunting kennels following a track ahead which eventually passes a house beside the Castle Brook, said to have been an inn serving early travellers. Shortly the track joins a metal road.

Follow the road to the right then turn immediately left still following the old sunken turnpike route now signed as a public footpath. At a tarmac lane turn left through the Deep Dean Valley for about half a mile to reach a bridleway on the right, which ascends through mixed woodland to the slopes of Howle Hill. Where the path levels beyond the trees do not miss a sharp turn left to follow a path going in a straight line across fields. Firstly cross the stile beside a gate, then a further stile ahead and walk across a large field to a gap in the hedge. From here head towards the right of a small wooded hillfort which is a rectangular Iron Age site standing at over 600 feet. It commands a panoramic view in clear weather of the Malvern Hills, Forest of Dean, Black Mountains and overlooks the Wye Valley.

Continue ahead along a farm track leading to a road opposite Great Howle Farm. Follow this road to the right and bear right at the crossroads following the signs to the Crown Inn.

The Crown Inn

This is a restored stone pub dating from the mid 1830's set in a hollow. It attracts customers from a wide area. Once Whitbread's, the star beers are now Wadsworth 6X and Marstons Pedigree though there is also a good selection of bottled beers and lagers too. It is a busy pub with no nasty gizmos to spoil the tranquility. Carpeted, comfortable and clean the Crown promises 'Not fast food but good food served fast'.

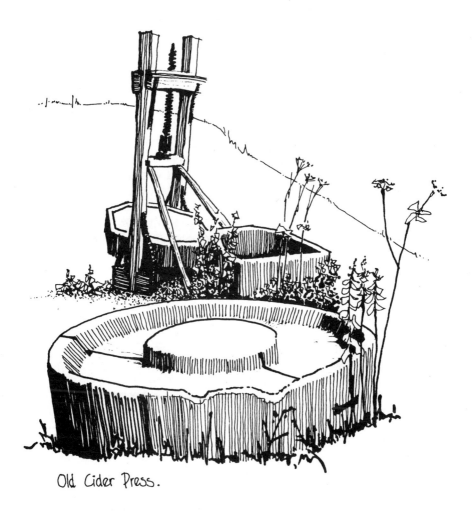

Old Cider Press.

The chalked menu is invariably toothsome and at random I list just a few of the dishes on offer, salmon surprise, rump steak with onion rings, chicken curry, steak and kidney as well as lots of snacks, fish and three veggie dishes. The sweets are equally innovative. The wine list is minimalist, limited to a couple of cheap and cheerful reds and whites.

Decor is easy on the eye with a few hunting prints, shining copper and brass bits and pieces, and there is plenty of parking.

Return

From the inn retrace your steps as far as the house called Old Barn. Here turn right to follow a winding tarmac lane past houses and cottages. Beyond a Victorian Chapel proceed along a signed bridleway on the right leading to a cottage then down a delightful leaf strewn sunken lane.

At a cottage named Still Meadow the waymarked route of the Wye Valley Walk is joined, which is followed from here to Hill Farm as described. Turn right and follow the way-marked route to Rose Cottage, then turn sharp left over a stile, cross a steeply sloping field and bear right down a track to a series of stiles. Keep to the right hand side of the next meadow to reach a stile leading onto the road at Coughton.

Turn left along the road for a few yards and beyond a collection of barns go right as indicated by the arrows, gently ascend through gates and fields to the thick woods of Chase Hill. Enter the woodlands by a gate and continue up a steep rocky path to the top of the hill, where the path skirts the single ramparts of another Iron Age hillfort. The path becomes wider overlooking a scenic valley before returning to Hill Farm. Now leave the Wye valley Walk, turn left and return to Fernbank Road.

8. KERNE BRIDGE

7½ mile walk from Hom Green, Ross-on-Wye to the Inn on the Wye, Walford.

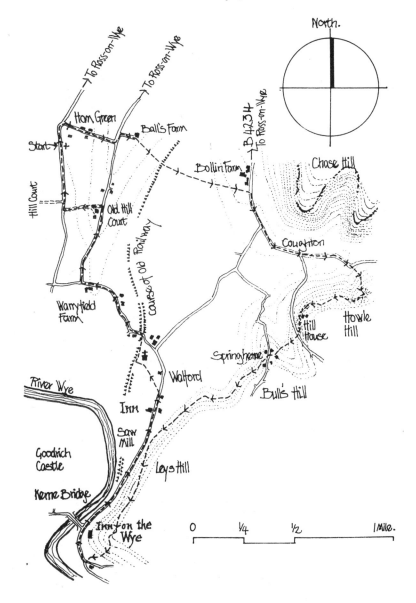

This is a superb section of the Wye Valley Walk across the steep slopes of Howle, Bull's and Ley's Hills lying to the south of Ross-on-Wye. A gentler stretch is first followed through low lying meadows from the quiet hamlet of Hom Green. The pub is two thirds of the way round, at Kerne Bridge, a delightful little spot above the Wye with excellent views of Goodrich Castle and the river.

Route

Cars may be parked outside the small Hom Green Church (GR 579221) which is still within the parish of Ross. This church, built in 1903, is about to be restored. Facing the church turn left along the road towards Ross, and just beyond Hom House turn right up a pretty lane with an interesting selection of cottages. At the junction bear left and enjoy the views of the the hills. Take the footpath on the right to Ball's Farm. Continue ahead through fields, gates and stiles to the railway embankment, all that now remains of the scenic Ross to Monmouth Railway, unfortunately closed in 1964. The path leads over the disused track into a meadow and ahead there is a stile almost hidden by undergrowth. Further stiles and gates lead through the next fields before keeping to the right of Bollin Farm, and between the farm buildings and the line of pylons to join the Ross to Coleford road.

Cross the road, turn right and walk on the pavement to the next junction, where the Howle Hill turn is taken through the hamlet of Coughton. Continue left at the next fork till passing Coughton Farm and the old mill. The distinctive waymarks of the Wye Valley Walk lead from here to Kerne Bridge. On the right the path leads uphill through fields, over stiles and along lanes to a stone dwelling on Howle Hill. Turn right along a pleasant track overlooking Chase Hill; it bears right passing an assortment of buildings before reaching the road beside Hill House.

Cross the stile opposite where the path descends to a delightful valley. A brook is crossed before a step ascent leads to cottages at Spring Herne on Bulls Hill, where a public footpath to Walford is followed. In early spring the banks of the path are covered in snowdrops, and in autumn the dried leaves rustle under foot. At Bramble Bank Cottage on Leys Hill the waymarked path continues along a track where a great variety of wild flowers grow, above the riverside village of Walford with its church, inn and school. As the path descends to the road opposite the sawmill, keep left following the Wye Valley Walk leading uphill, passing scattered cottages.

At the top of the hill pass between the cottage and converted barn then along the main track for 100 yards where the Wye Valley Walk turns sharp right, following a narrow winding path which gradually descends to the road. Cross the road, bear right still following the waymarked trail to Kerne Bridge. Opposite is the Inn on the Wye.

Flanesford Priory, Kerne Bridge & Goodrich Castle

The Inn on the Wye

The Inn on the Wye has been recently and quite splendidly rescued from oblivion. A great deal has been spent on total renovation and the inn, in the majestic shadow of Goodrich Castle, now offers several bars with commercial sounding names to do with poaching, coaching and the stabling of horses. Old items of horse tack and other country artefacts embellish this country theme. There are rooms for drinking, dining, dancing, even getting hitched and a little games area with a pool table and a couple of fruit machines waiting to eat small change. Muzak pours reassuringly.

The menus are interesting with tasty soups and snacks as well as serious evening food. Children and veggies are not discriminated against either, and there is a wine list of modest pretensions. The beers include the reliable Wadsworth 6X, Flowers, Boddingtons, Boston and Murphy's. The Inn on the Wye intends to appeal to a wide range of clientele and in the evenings music from Blues to Folk is offered as well as Karaoke and pub quizzes We lunched outdoors on a fine autumn day and after we'd tucked into our snacks followed with a cafetiere of good strong coffee, enjoyed the green and hilly views around, the world seemed at peace.

Return

From the inn either turn right along the Ross road to the attractive stone bridge built in 1828 and keep to this side of the river for half a mile to the saw mill, or more pleasantly retrace your steps to the saw mill along the Wye Valley Walk to avoid this stretch of busy road. Proceed through the village of Walford with its garage and inn, before the road veers to the left cross a stile. Here a signed footpath leads across the field and a brook by a wooden bridge to the thirteenth century church of St. Michael. Keep to the left of this solid building surrounded by yew trees. Iron swing gates lead out of the churchyard, and a narrow overgrown path, beside the disused railway track, leads onto Hom Green Road, followed to the left.

Warryfield Cottage and Farm are passed on opposite sides of the road before turning right to follow a tarmac lane to Old Hill Court. Beyond this black and white house turn left along the drive also serving as a right of way to Hom Green. On meeting the lower road turn right, passing the elegant Hill Court, built in the late seventeenth century. Within a few hundred yards you are back at Hom Green Church.

Kerne Bridge

9. GOODRICH CHURCH

6 mile walk from Welsh Bicknor to Ye Hostelrie, Goodrich.

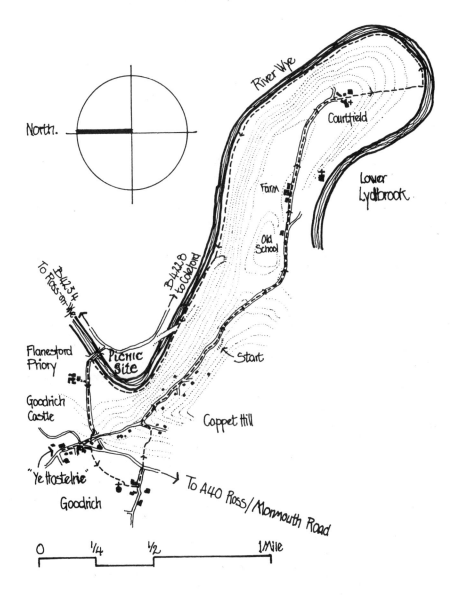

High above the Wye stands the compact village of Goodrich with its historic castle, church and priory. This easy ramble leads through the remote riverside parish of Welsh Bicknor, where an interesting route through the Courtfield estate joins the Wye Valley Walk. At Goodrich there is ample time to visit the mock Gothic inn, the ruins of the Norman castle and the thirteenth century church of St. Giles.

Route

Cars may be parked at a small disused quarry (GR 583184) on the right hand side of the road from Goodrich to Welsh Bicknor. Walk along the road for nearly a quarter of a mile, and after passing a stone cottage, once the school, fork left along the private road to Glen Wye, also a public footpath to the riverside. Cottages and farm buildings are passed before reaching Glen Wye, where the footpath continues ahead with the monastic buildings of Courtfield on the right. The path becomes stony as it descends to a field gate, and follows along the left hand side of field to join the Wye Valley Walk at the riverside.

Opposite are the wooded hills of the Forest of Dean above the once industrial village of Lower Lydbrook. Turn left along the waymarked walk, a pleasant route through meadows, mixed woodland and arable fields leading to the handsome Kerne Bridge. Along the latter section the ruins of Goodrich Castle and the barns of Flanesford Priory are in sight. In mid river you will notice several small islands, always a popular nesting site for swans.

At Kerne Bridge leave the Wye Valley Walk and turn left along the road to Goodrich. Keep to the pavement passing the entrance to renovated Flanesford where all that remains of the original Augustinian Priory, founded in the fourteenth century, are the refectory, barns and fish ponds. Before the Dry Bridge, an unusual stone arch spanning the road, bear left up the path and steps, and turn right to cross the bridge. Follow the road down to the shop, castle and inn at Goodrich.

Ye Hostelrie

Ye Hostelrie with its strange grey stone pinnacles and turrets is at first glance something out of a Hitchcock movie. Once inside it assumes normality and is in fact a neat pub, gas fired 'logs' in one bar, and a side room, where ramblers may rest awhile and enjoy a drink and a snack. There is also a pink dining room.

The extensive menu includes ten starters, steaks, grills, and fish courses. Baguettes are good too. Wine is available by the glass or bottle and there is an ample range of good beers and ciders including Marstons Pedigree, Wye Valley, Cask Aged, Tetleys, Strongbow and Scrumpy Jack. The bars

"Ye Hostelrie", Goodrich.

are beamed and floors are tiles and carpeted. A variety of 'amusing' prints hang on the walls together with horse brasses. Ye Hostelrie is a comfortable respite for the happy wanderer and locals say it is worth a try in the evening too.

Return

After rest and refreshments, retrace your way back to the castle entrance, where a well signed lane leads to the historic remains of Goodrich Castle. Now in the care of English Heritage, it is open at all reasonable times, and is well worth the detour. Return to the shop and pass the Primary School, where a signed footpath on the right leads across playing fields to a gate. Bear left here and follow this path over a shallow brook, through fields and a swing gate before reaching the churchyard.

Dedicated to St. Giles, the church has a slender fourteenth century spire. If the key can be obtained there are items of interest to inspect, including a communion cup given to the church by Dean Swift, the Irish author of Gulliver's Travels, in memory of his grandfather, vicar of this parish during the Civil War. Leave the church by the path on the south west side, leading between fields and high stone walls of the Old Vicarage. At the road turn left to the junction, cross the Goodrich Road to reach the stile opposite signed 'Coppet Hill and YHA'. Keep ahead up the hilly field and head for the stile in the corner. This leads onto a narrow sunken path with a flight of stone steps. At the tarmac lane, the top of the northern end of Coppet Hill, there are delightful views of the Wye Valley.

Turn left along the lane which shortly joins the Welsh Bicknor Road which is followed to the right, passing several houses and cottages built into the hillside. In the adjacent woodland, winter ramblers will notice squirrels' drays and pigeons' nests in leafless trees. Beside the road is a disused Victorian well inscribed 'Waste Not Want Not'. Continue for another few hundred yards to return to the disused quarry.

English Bicknor from Eastbach Farm

10. LOWER LYDBROOK

OS Sheet 162

7 mile walk from English Bicknor to the Anchor Inn.

NORTH

Welsh Bicknor
Church & Y.H.A.

River Wye

Old Railway

Paper
Factory

Picnic Site

Lower Lydbrook

B4228
To Ross-On-Wye

Anchor Inn

Rosemary
Topping

START

English Bicknor

Bicknor Court

Eastbach Farm

Hangerberry
Wood

B4228
To Coleford

Court

Barn

Birchmarsh

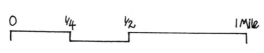

0   ¼   ½   1 Mile

The village of English Bicknor lies mid-way between the River Wye and the Forest of Dean. The twelfth century church of St. Mary stands within the ramparts of an early Norman Castle where the wooded mound of the motte can still be seen. This walk is strenuous in places but easy to follow as most of the route is waymarked along forest trails and the Wye Valley Walk. It starts from English Bicknor where a twisting metalled lane leads through remote countryside to join a forest trail which meanders down to Lower Lydbrook and the Anchor Inn.

Route

At English Bicknor there is parking near the church (GR 582158) and a bus service from Coleford. Cross the main Ross to Coleford Road, after a few yards, turn left along a quiet lane to Eastbach with its rendered farmhouse and attractive Court surrounded by a high stone wall. Take the right hand fork leading around this building and follow the lane until reaching Birchmarsh Cottages, where a field path on the left, beyond the cottages, is followed towards a modernised barn. Keep to the right of the barn, and cross the field gate on the right where the way ahead closely follows the right hand hedge ascending to over 600 feet before reaching a solid stile. Here catch your breath and enjoy the exhilarating views of the windswept landscape. Continue ahead to a gate leading into the forest, and turn left along the sparsely waymarked forest trail. For the less robust, an alternative route from Birchmarsh Cottages is to follow the lane past a large old milestone to beyond the next cottage where a signed footpath on the left shortly joins the waymarked trail.

The yellow arrowed path leads through Hangerberry Wood with its beech, oak and larch trees, and bears left at a clearing overlooking Lower Lydbrook. Scars left from the iron, tin and coal mining of previous industrial days can be seen below. It is difficult to imagine that this valley was criss-crossed with tramways, railways and viaducts to transport these products. The waymarked trail continues along a narrow rocky path descending steeply to a lane followed to the left, passing several cottages before twisting and turning through a stand of delightful beech trees. Be careful to follow the waymarked footpath leading out of the woods and across fields. At a stile bear right to meet the road at Lower Lydbrook where a right turn will lead directly to the Anchor Inn about 100 yards away. It stands opposite an attractive cottage connected with the famous eighteenth century actress, Sarah Siddons.

The Anchor Inn

The Anchor, dating it is alleged from the 1450s, is a find in an area not brimming with good pubs. Sympathetically restored by a caring landlord it fulfills all the necessary requirements. The food is tasty and much is home made, the decor is easy on the eyes and the furnishing comfortable. A wood burning stove and several wall heaters keep the temperature in winter at a reasonable level, and easy listening background music provided by the likes of Jim Reeves is not intrusive.

An experienced chef offers excellent fare, soup - good rich cockle warming stuff, and homemade game and brandy paté, the curry and rice is tasty and attractively presented. Other attractions include vegetarian dishes, lemon sole and steaks as well as freshly prepared sandwiches. The beers include a creamy Free Miners Ale, Toby, Caffreys and Stowfords Cider. Ordinary wine is available by bottle and glass.

Apart from the exposed beams, carpeted floors and the usual pub furniture, there are lots of pictures adorning the whitewashed walls. There is also a well laid out dining room for the more serious diner, with an interesting menu, and children and animals (under control) are actively encouraged. Parking is adequate.

Return

Retrace your steps back to the last stile but continue along the road to a pleasant picnic site beside the River Wye. Turn left, following the Coleford Road, until shortly reaching a stile, the start of a signed riverside path leading through fields and bracken clad banks, ideal habitat for swans and wild ducks. On the opposite side of the Wye stands the modern church of Welsh Bicknor. It was rebuilt just over a century ago in the Norman style, next to a rambling old vicarage, now a Youth Hostel. The path comes close to a large paperworks, and after crossing a brook, leads to a large disused railway bridge, where the Wye Valley Walk is joined. On this walk it is only followed for a short stretch under the bridge then along the banks of the Wye with the wooded conical shape hill of Rosemary Topping ahead. a stile and a flight of steps lead onto the remains of the Ross to Monmouth railway track. Leave the Wye Valley Walk here by turning sharp left along the track to follow a waymarked path to Common Grove. A steep climb across hilly fields and over a well defined section of Offa's Dyke is followed with the aid of yellow arrows, these lead through more fields above great Collins Grove to arrive at a tarmac lane beside Grove Cottage. Follow this quiet lane where a gradual uphill haul, keeping left at the junction, leads to a row of cottages. Beyond these dwellings turn left through a swing gate, over a rough paddock, through the school yard to arrive back at English Bicknor Church.

English   The Bicknor Churches   Welsh

11. SEVEN SISTERS

7½ mile walk from Symonds Yat Rock to the Saracen's Head.

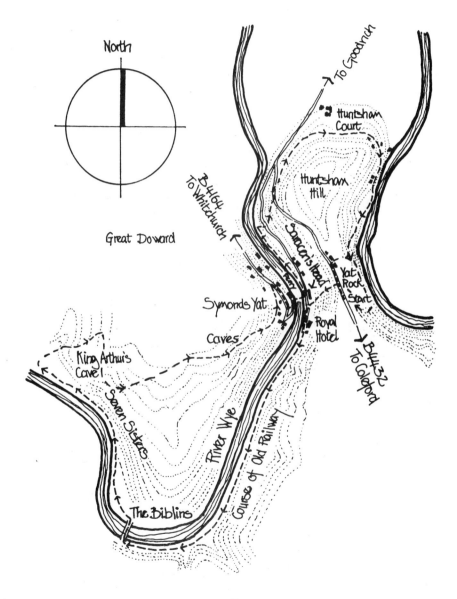

Symonds Yat is the is the most popular place for sightseers and walkers in the Wye Valley. The scattered village lies along the east and west banks of the River Wye where cottages, inns and hotels are attractively built in the steeply wooded slopes of this scenic gorge. There is parking on the east side at the Yat Rock car park, the start of this strenuous but interesting walk. The route offering splendid and varied views follows waymarked paths and the Wye Valley Walk descending to cross the river and climb steeply to King Arthur's Cave and the Seven Sisters before re-crossing the Wye to reach the Saracen's Head. A shorter return around Huntsham Hill leads back to the Yat Rock. The ferry operates most of the year except during mid winter and adverse weather conditions. If in doubt ring 01600 890435

River Wye from Yat Rock

Route

From the Symonds Yat Rock car park (GR 565159) the yellow arrows of a waymarked path are easily located leading from the log cabin. The path descends the 400 feet down to the riverside, zig-zagging through trees and down slippery steps. At the river bank by the Royal Hotel turn left where the Wye Valley Walk follows the route of the dismantled remains of the Ross to Monmouth Railway, surely one of the prettiest lines in the country when it operated between 1873 and 1964. The rapids are soon reached, a favourite stretch of water for canoeists to practise their skills. On the opposite side of the bank is the site of the New Weir iron works, a forge which existed for many centuries and was in use up to the early nineteenth century.

A mile further downstream the steeply wooded and rocky gorge widens at the Biblins, where a suspension bridge takes the walker across the river. The Wye Valley Walk continues to the left along the riverside below the tall rocky outcrops known as the Seven Sisters and disused quarries. Take care not to miss a turning on the right which follows another forest path, clearly waymarked with yellow arrows. It follows a steep, rocky path, winding above quarries and boulders before reaching King Arthur's Cave, where traces of prehistoric man and animals were discovered in 1870.

Having explored the cave, follow the waymarks through the trees to a magnificent viewpoint at the top of the Seven Sisters. From here continue to the sandstone quarry, where the forest trail veers right across a mixed woodland with, in season, several spices of fungi. Cross the first forest track and continue until another track is met. Turn left and descend to more caves at a point where the rushing of the rapids may be heard. Keep ahead along the track to a tarmac lane, then bear right towards the river. Here turn right and shortly take a footpath on the left which leads to the ferry crossing, operated by the Saracen's Head on the opposite bank. hail for the ferryman who pulls the boat across by means of a cable and collects your payment for a soothing and restful crossing.

The Saracen's Head

This old free house is nicely positioned by the Wye in a busy stretch of the valley with guest houses, hotels and pubs lining both banks of the river. Once a cider mill, the Saracen's Head is now much changed but still popular. There are two bars, one a basic place with a pool table and fruit machines, the other a comfortable dining room with scrubbed pine tables. Gas powered 'logs' keep it warm in winter while in summer customers can sit on the grass outside, watching the ferryman (the barman) ply his ancient trade, while listening to Vivaldi on the pub stereo.

The menu is packed with interesting food. The brie, courgette and almond crumble is worth trying. Also listed are homemade pies, soups, paté, toasted sandwiches and ploughman's. Veggies too are catered for. The service is friendly and prompt. Decor includes framed cigarette cards and black and white photos of ancients posing with animals.

The beer offers a decent range which includes Theakers Old Peculiar - a sensational soft black brew, and other guest beers which should satisfy the most demanding Real Aler. There is the usual litany of lagers and ciders. But don't over do it - the rest of this walk is fairly strenuous.

At present the Saracen's Head closes, except for weekends in December and January.

Return

Rejoin the Wye Valley Walk beside the inn. Continue right along the riverside leaving the picturesque village to the upper ferry. Turn right, cross the road, go up the slope and follow the waymarked walk through woods and along forest tracks. Some fine views will be enjoyed of Huntsham Court, Goodrich Church and fern clad slopes of Coppet Hill. Notice the huge boulders of conglomerate rock, known locally as pudding stone, but do not miss a left turn down steps leading to the riverside.

A steep sunken lane leads past several ruined cottages, abandoned perhaps because of sliding boulders. The thick woods are a delight; a blend of holly, spindle, chestnut, mosses, ferns, fungi and old man's beard. At the riverside the 400 feet high Yat Rock comes into view, as one bears right away from the Wye. The ascent along the Wye Valley Walk is followed up steps, around bends, then veers left along a forest track until reaching a sign-posted junction where the Wye Valley Walk continues. Our way goes right up to Yat Rock. This narrow steep track eventually leads to several cottages, where a right turn leads to the road beside disused lime kilns.

Follow the road to the left back to the Yat Rock car park. If you still have any energy, walk over the wooden bridge you have just passed beneath, this leads to the famous view of the horseshoe bend. Then enjoy well earned refreshments at the log cabin.

12. REDBROOK BRIDGE

6 mile walk from the Kymin to the Boat Inn.

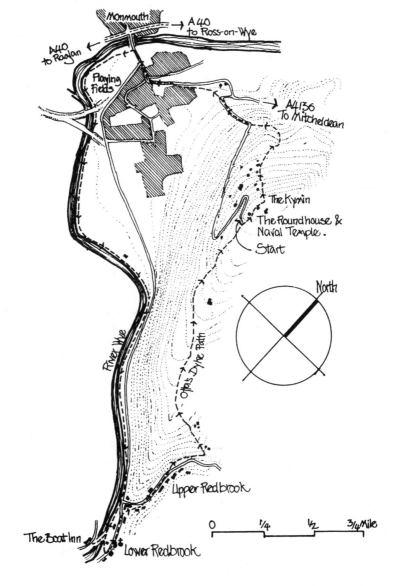

This is a splendid and scenic walk in the heart of the Wye Valley leading from the Kymin, a beauty spot standing at over 800 feet offering outstanding views over Monmouth and the Welsh hills. The route is easy to follow, along two waymarked routes, Offa's Dyke Path and the Wye Valley Walk. However, a long steep climb back to the Kymin awaits you after a welcome pause for refreshment at Redbrook Bridge. The Kymin has been managed by the National Trust since the beginning of this century. The site dates back to 1793 when a group of Monmouth gentlemen created the pleasure grounds, and built the Roundhouse. In 1800 the Naval Temple was erected, commemorating sixteen famous English admirals. Two years later Lord Nelson visited the temple and said that the view was one of the finest he had ever seen.

The Roundhouse on The Kymin.

Route

The walk begins at the National Trust car park at the Kymin (GR 528126). Follow the yellow arrows and white acorns, marking Offa's Dyke Path, which leads past the unusual Naval Temple, the white Roundhouse and the magnificent viewpoint. The route continues slightly to the left down a rocky path which disappears into thick woodland. On meeting a 'Private Road', turn immediately right across open land before entering further woods. A tarmac lane is soon reached, descending towards Monmouth until a waymarked path through fields and woodland leads to the outskirts of Monmouth.

This historic Welsh town of Monmouth grew around the Norman Castle and where the River Monnow joins the Wye. It has many attractive Georgian buildings and associations with Henry V, Nelson and Charles Rolls of Rolls Royce fame. Turn left along the road and immediately before the Wye Bridge turn sharp left to leave Offa's Dyke Path and join the Wye Valley Walk, waymarked with leaping salmons. From this point the path closely follows the banks of the River Wye for about three miles to Redbrook. Firstly it skirts the playing fields of Monmouth School before going under a disused railway bridge of the old Ross to Monmouth Railway, in operation from 1873 to 1965, then the path continues beneath the dismantled viaduct of the Wye Valley Railway which carried passengers from 1876 to 1956 along the route between Monmouth and Chepstow.

The remaining two miles to Redbrook are along a most delightful stretch of the Wye. In June we counted sixteen different wild flowers including masses of comfrey, campions and vetches. Dragonflies too were enjoying the summer sun above the rippling currents of the river. Timeless scenes constantly appeared as multicoloured cows waded in and drank from the cool water, a clutch of ducklings swam around their mother, and fishermen either waist-high in water or sitting more comfortably in a dinghy were hoping to net a Wye salmon.

Before reaching Redbrook the railway bridge comes into view, at the village the way-marked path leads onto the road. At a former pub the path goes right to rejoin the riverbank to Redbrook Bridge. Walk over this old rusty iron bridge, another reminder of the railway age, but now serving only as a footbridge. In its shadow stands the Boat Inn, where refreshments may be obtained before an energetic return.

The Boat Inn

The Boat, in several well known guides, is situated on the sunny right hand bank of the River Wye and is the only Welsh pub in this book. It is a tiny and interesting old inn with plenty of beams, and a quarry tiled floor. A dart board hangs on one wall and two sweet smelling wood burning stoves keep the old place cosy during the damp days of winter. There are a few amusing pictures and sketches to examine in the main lounge.

Food and refreshment are good and the beer selection includes a host of beers, with funny names like Sneck Lifter, Cocker Hoop, Red Fox, Tanners Jack and Free Miner. Lagers and ciders cater for more ordinary palates and vin ordinaire is available in bottle and glass. A list of hedgerow wines is also offered. The menu contains sufficient variety and we personally appreciate the accent on unusual vegetarian dishes. Perennial favourites like Ploughman's with plenty of good English cheese and homemade soups satisfy most ramblers but the Javanese Pork and Orange, the Nine Vegetable Chilli and the Boozy Bbeef are attractive options on a cold day.

Evening Caterwauling around the Joanna is encouraged and pub quizzes are regularly arranged.

This is a quiet spot with the Wye silently slipping by a few feet away and dark trees growing up to the skyline. Cars may be left in the car park (in England!) over the river.

Return

Leave the Boat and retrace your steps back over the bridge, but turn right, then leave through the inn's car park to reach the road in the centre of Redbrook. This village once boasted a busy industrial past of iron foundries, mills, a brewery, a railway, a tramway and barges on the Wye. Tinplate works remained until 1961, but the dirt and dust of the past has left Redbrook a quiet place with just a few interesting sites and memories. Rejoin Offa's Dyke Path by turning left, then past the church, built in 1873 by J.D. Seddon, who also designed the unique Italian church at Hoarwithy. Shortly bear right up a wide track, leading between cottages and derelict mills to join the Newland Road at the unusual incline tram bridge. Follow the road to the right for a few hundred yards then bear left and steeply ascend the hills of the Forest of Dean. At the top a farm overlooks a lovely wooded valley, where the route veers left along an ancient shady lane. Extensive views of the Forest of Dean and the Wye Valley may be seen. At a converted barn leave the lane, turn right across the stile, where the path leads across fields and stiles, to reach the Kymin car park by a pair of iron gates.

PATHS and PUBS of the WYE VALLEY

The Authors

Heather Hurley as a Voluntary Countryside Warden in the Wye Valley and Chairman of the Ross Civic Society's Rights of Way Committee, has first hand experience of keeping the miles of rights of way open and in use by the general public. She is the author of several publications on walking and local history which she has personally researched and written. Her hobbies include riding, and gardening.

Jon Hurley lectures, writes and broadcasts on the subject of wine. He has also written prose, plays and poetry. He enjoys walking, golf, foreign travel and, like Heather, takes a keen interest in gardening and the countryside.

Titles by Jon and Heather Hurley

The Wicked Wind, 1980

Forest of Dean Pubs, 1981

Wyedean Walks, 1st Edition, 1983

100 Herefordshire Pubs, 1984

Paths and Pubs of the Wye Valley, 1st Edition, 1986

Wine for Game and Fish, 1986

Rambles and Refreshments, 1988

Family Walks in the Wye Valley, 1989

The Wine Label Album, 1990

The Old Roads of South Herefordshire, 1992

A History of the River Crossing at Wilton, 1993

The Wye Valley Walk, 1994

Thomas Blake, 1996

Fownhope Parish Paths, 1996

Historic Harewood, 1996

Five Walks from Ross-on-Wye, 1997

Ross-on-Wye Heritage Trail, 1997